Sweetmaking for Children

Margaret Powell

SWEETMAKING
for Children

Revised Edition

illustrations by
Karen Heywood

A Piccolo Original
Piccolo Books

First published 1972 by Pan Books Ltd,
Cavaye Place, London SW10 9PG
6th printing 1979
7th printing (revised) 1983
8th printing 1983
© Margaret Powell 1972, 1983
ISBN 0 330 26963 1
Printed in Great Britain by
Hunt Barnard Ltd, Aylesbury, Bucks

Contents

1 Why bother?

Today there are more sweets in the shops than
ever before and in greater variety, so it may seem
strange that I should bother to write a book on
how you can make your own.

I suppose it's because when I was young I got a
lot of fun out of it. After that, much to my
surprise, my three boys were always on at me to
let them have a go and when I did they not only
enjoyed making them and of course eating them,
but got very good at it. Now there are my
grandchildren, most of whom live a long way
from me, unfortunately, but they come and visit
me from time to time. When they were very
young I used to make sweets before they came.
They liked them so much that as they grew older
they asked me to show them how I made them.
Now, when they come to see me or I go to them
I'm expected to have a new recipe to try with
them and I'm glad to say they often have one to
show me.

So, since three generations of my family have
enjoyed making sweets, I feel that it's an art that
doesn't go out of date, and that those of you
who haven't yet tried may like doing it. I hope
you may find that the things I've learnt over the
years will be of help to you. Perhaps, too, I may

have a few new ideas for those of you who are already good at making sweets.

One of the difficulties you're going to find is getting your mother to let you use her kitchen. Don't be too hard on her over this as it's a place she takes a pride in, and she may well not want you messing it up and using her precious utensils. You may have to choose your moment carefully to get her to agree. I remember that was so with my mother. When my brothers and sisters and I wanted to make sweets we used to get my young sister to ask. She had big eyes and a pretty face and could look pathetic and appealing. I was a great hefty, clumsy-looking child, the sort that was likely to cause havoc in any kitchen. I also looked as if I'd eaten too many sweets already and unkind people sometimes said so. It wasn't true because I only got a halfpenny a week pocket money and the number of sweets that could buy wouldn't put on much weight!

If we were lucky, mother was in a good mood and father was in work so there was plenty of sugar in the larder, and we'd be allowed to have a go. As mother has since said to me and as I have found out myself, it's a good way of keeping children occupied happily all afternoon. Also she felt we were doing something constructive. She was a great one for this. I remember her giving me a duster and making the business of dusting round a room into a game. This game got bigger and longer when she gave me a broom and a dustpan and brush. Then came the game of making beds and doing the shopping. Of course, after a few days doing this, it stopped being a game and became a chore; mother had got me helping her with the housework. She was a very clever woman.

Sweetmaking, though, has never become a chore for me. I love it just as I love most cooking. I know it sounds a funny thing to say, but I believe that to do anything really well you've got to put a bit of love into it. There are, of course, jobs that just *have* to be done, but to make up for these there are the others which you enjoy and which you do better because of the happiness you get out of doing them.

My oldest son Harry started with sweetmaking, then he saw me making cheese straws out of the odds and ends of pastry I'd got left and tried these. He became better at them than I was and could fit them into the rings he made to go round them, without breaking any. He eventually became a very good cook indeed and

9

(don't laugh!) a very good tailor and dressmaker. He makes a lot of his own and his wife's clothes, although in his job he's an atomic scientist.

I think that this shows that sweetmaking is not just for girls, just as there are a lot of boys' toys and games that girls enjoy. I must say one of the things that riles me and yet unfortunately is true is that men often make the best chefs.

I hope when you read this book you're going to want to make sweets and you may feel like starting right away. But as I've said you will probably have to be patient because your mother's using the kitchen for the everyday cooking that keeps you alive and, let's face it, sweets won't do that! You won't normally be able to make them when you come back from school because there isn't time, and sweetmaking does take time. I think Saturday afternoons are best or when you are on holiday. You need plenty of time to get things ready, follow the instructions carefully and prepare and cook the sweets. The ingredients cost money and you won't want to waste things if you can help it. I remember my boys once making some almond creams; they asked, 'How much almond essence, Mum?' 'Oh just a few drops,' I told them. They decided I was being stingy so put in a whole teaspoonful. Well, of course it tasted awful and had to be thrown away. Even our ginger cat, who loved sweets and ate practically anything, walked away after one sniff.

However, I must point out that though you may not be as foolish as my sons, you'll make

10

mistakes, and you will have some failures even when you are sure you've followed my instructions carefully. I've been cooking for over forty years and it still happens to me. The other day I made a sponge cake, and I pride myself on the way I make them. I did it the same way as I've always done and yet when I got it out of the oven it was as flat as a pancake. My husband said, 'Oh, making biscuits are you?' He was very sorry he'd said it afterwards, I made sure of that! I was disappointed, but it hasn't put me off making sponge cakes. So I hope that if things don't turn out right the first time, you won't stop trying.

There's one other thought that strikes me. I've said that the ingredients cost money. I also told you that I only got a halfpenny a week pocket money when I was young. I'm sure you get more, probably much more than that, so offer to pay for at least part of what you are likely to use. It's only fair and it will also mean that your mother will be prepared to lend you her kitchen more often, particularly if you give it back to her as clean and tidy as it was when she lent it to you.

2 What things will I need?

For every job that is done around the house, certain tools are needed and, as I'm sure you will have noticed, it's the same with cooking. In the kitchen these are generally called utensils but I still prefer to call them my tools, probably because when I was in domestic service as a cook they were the tools of my trade.

I think you will find that most of the things I mention your mother will have and will let you use. But let me warn you, she may well say 'You can't have that.' Don't be hurt or cross with her. Every housewife has certain utensils that she treasures. They have become part of her and she wouldn't like even her own mother to use them. Try to understand why. Probably you yourself feel the same about certain things of your own.

Once you are in the kitchen and before you begin anything else, choose the utensils you know you will need and lay them out on the table in front of you. In other words, have everything ready before you begin.

I shall always remember my first job as a kitchen-maid. This was in the days when rich people had a lot of servants. I was told that it was one of my jobs to lay out the cook's table. It was a huge wooden table and the top was scrubbed white and kept that way, as I know well because it was my job to scrub it. I started to lay it out, putting a couple of knives here, a few tablespoons there, three or four basins around them and a pastry board and rolling pin in the middle. Then I thought I had finished. Fortunately the cook was out because when the under-housemaid saw what I'd done she burst out laughing. 'She'll need that ten times over,' she said and, being a kind girl, she showed me what to do. There were knives of every kind, little ones for paring, coring knives, medium-sized sharp ones for cutting up meat, large carvers and a chopper; teaspoons, tablespoons, a large metal spoon which gave weights and measures, wooden spoons of all sizes; basins of all sizes; a pastry board and rolling pin, of course, pastry brushes, graters, wire sieves and hair sieves. There was a place for everything and everything had to be in its place. And there was a reason for it, because cooks work fast and with a purpose. Things must be ready at the right time and there is nothing that

makes a cook crosser than not having the thing to hand which she needs next.

Well, of course, you haven't got to work in quite such an elaborate way, but even with sweetmaking there are moments when something needs to be done quickly; if you're not ready your mixture can spoil. Particularly remember to grease your tins beforehand, and try and see that everything is ready for its right moment. I know you'll want to handle the ingredients as soon as possible, but don't rush at them.

Here is a list of the implements you may need: kitchen scales, heavy aluminium or steel saucepans (sugar can stick on enamel ones), some wooden spoons for stirring and, if possible, one of those large metal ones with measures marked on them – a jug or glass with measures

printed on it may also be useful. You'll need baking tins for pouring sweets into that have to set, a rolling pin for crushing sugar or nuts, a fairly large pastry board, a big basin and one or two smaller ones, a sharp knife and, if you have one, a sieve for sifting icing sugar – if you haven't, a large wire strainer will do. You may need a grater for various peels, a pastry brush (because lots of sweets need to be brushed over with white of egg or icing sugar), plenty of greaseproof paper and a set of round cutters, though you can use egg cups or other shapes; a pair of scissors is always handy (they needn't be sharp). When my children were young, cutters were made of tin, but now you can buy them made of plastic – they are colourful and cheap and very easy to keep clean. If you go to a fairly large hardware shop, they will have all kinds of plastic cutters in the shape of stars, half-moons, hearts and diamonds. If you are thinking of packing a box with sweets as a present for somebody, it's well worth buying a few of these pretty cutters. Finally, and very important, make sure you have a damp cloth for wiping your hands on when they get sticky.

Like the things that were laid out on the cook's table in my time, it sounds a lot, but unlike my cook you won't need them all at the same time. Your mother is almost certain to use most of them every day of her life. What I've done is to tell you the things you'll need if you try *every* recipe in the book. Do not worry if your mother does not have all the things I have mentioned. I'm sure that you will find that she has the really essential things, like basins and pans, spoons and pastry board. I like using the old tools that I have had for years. I use an old pair of scales with weights, not the spring balance sort, though they are probably as good. It's just that I'm fond of my old-fashioned scales, and anyway, they refuse to wear out. I don't use a thermometer, I just judge it – in the case of toffee I drop a little piece into cold water. If it sets quickly the toffee is ready. If it doesn't set, then it needs to boil for a longer time.

The same with cutters. If you have only one or two in the kitchen, it's very easy to manage. You can cut shapes with almost anything, small glasses, egg cups and glass lids. Or you can use your imagination and design your own shapes, cutting them out with a knife.

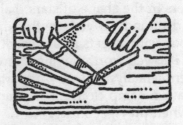

If you haven't any salad- or olive-oil to grease the tins, then put a small piece of margarine in the tin and rub it round with a bit of greaseproof paper.

When you have to brown almonds, put them into the oven at a not too high heat; say Gas mark 3 to 4, Electricity 325°–350°F or 170°–180° C.

3 Watch it!

When you've persuaded your mother to let you borrow her kitchen, to lend you some of her utensils and give you some of the ingredients you will need, don't then try to 'shoo' her out of the kitchen. It's very probable that you are going to need her help and it's almost certain that she's going to insist on keeping an eye on you. Not, I hope, because she thinks you're going to misbehave but because she wants to make sure that you come to no harm. You see, you will be working with materials which have to reach a great heat, a very high temperature, and one spot on your skin will cause you a lot of pain. At boiling point sugar is much hotter than water and you know how that can scald you. On the other hand, don't be frightened when you're dealing with hot things, nervousness can cause accidents, so if you are ever a bit afraid call on your mother's help. As you get more experience so you will get more confidence.

My mother gave us five safety rules which she made us promise to keep before we were allowed to begin sweetmaking. I think they are as important today as they were fifty years ago.

The first is to be careful to make sure when you put pans or anything with a handle on the stove, that the handle is not sticking out over the edge of the stove.

It is so easy, if you do, to knock it over as you move by. On the other hand don't put it over another hot plate or jet because when you come to pick it up, even with gloves on, it may well burn your hands.

Talking about leaving the handles over the edge of the stove, I remember when I was a kitchen-maid it was one of my jobs to make some of the sauces to go with the various dishes. One evening the people I worked for were giving a dinner party for twelve very important people. Important for them that is. For the fish course we were serving turbot, an expensive fish, and preparing two sauces to go with it: Hollandaise and shrimp sauces.

The cook made the Hollandaise because it is more difficult and I did the shrimp. When the cook had finished hers she put it in a bowl and the bowl into a pan of hot water and left it with the handle outside the stove. As I went to look at my sauce I walked into the handle and knocked the lot on the floor. I was fortunate not to get it on my legs, which would have put me out of action for weeks. Cook was angry, but with herself, not me. She was a fair woman and knew it was her fault. It was too late for her to make any more so my shrimp sauce had to do. We expected to be in trouble from the lady of the house but the next day when she came down to the kitchen she said to the cook, 'That was a lovely shrimp sauce. The best I've ever tasted, thank you, cook.' I was very happy about what she said but the cook was cross. I was young at the time and I remember thinking how difficult it was to please older people. I wonder if you've ever found the same. Even if you have, still remember to keep those handles in!

The second thing mother told us was never to pick up anything that was hot without using oven gloves or an oven cloth. I suppose you will think this is unnecessary advice. 'I'd never do that,' you'll say to yourself. It's easy to forget, particularly when you are carrying dishes only a short distance. 'It's only got to go from there to there,' you'll think, but it's likely that if you hold it in your bare hands you'll end up either with blistered fingers or with what you're moving on the floor.

While I like food on hot plates, they can be a torture. Once, to earn a bit of extra money, I went to serve at a dinner party. When it came to the soup course I must have got some extra hot plates. There I was walking towards the table with them burning into my thumb and fingers. Well, of course, I got shaky and that spilled the hot soup on to my thumbs. I did the last few yards to the table at a gallop and put the plates, with relief, in front of the guests. One of them said, 'Thank you. It's the first time I've had tomato soup with thumb flavouring.' I felt awful at the time but when I told the other waitresses they all roared with laughter.

Mother's third rule only applies to those of you who cook by gas. It's a simple one. Make sure that when you turn on the tap the gas lights. Now in the old days when you had to use a match or a lighter this was easy to follow but today, with stoves that are supposed to light automatically when you turn the tap, things go wrong.

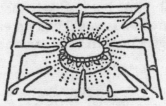

It happened to me recently. I put on a kettle, turned on the tap and went away. I came back expecting to find the kettle boiling. It wasn't even warm. The gas pilot light that feeds the jet had got clogged up and so the jet wasn't alight but was filling the room with dangerous fumes. It's a small thing but it needs watching. Also many people now use North Sea gas, which is all right except that it is difficult to regulate at the lowest heat and often blows out.

The fourth rule concerns the use of knives. (I don't say *sharp* knives because all knives should be sharp.) This rule is: always cut on a board and always slice downwards or away from you. I remember once when I was a girl, we were short of money so mother had to go out to work as a cleaner and I had to get the other children's breakfasts. I was cutting a loaf of bread towards me, the knife slipped and I got a gash in my hand between the thumb and the forefinger. I'd been told by a girl at school that this kind of cut could cause lockjaw. I was very frightened and I stood outside the front door shouting and moving my jaw up and down at the same time so that it wouldn't lock. What my friend said wasn't true and I must have looked a very funny sight.

Something similar, but more painful happened to my husband. For a time he worked as a butcher and he cut a piece of meat towards him and sliced the top of his finger off. It was only a small piece but nobody could discover it. I always joke about it and tell him it must have found its way into the sausages. He pretends to strangers that it's his war wound. Funny creatures, men!

If I haven't frightened you off sweetmaking for ever, here's a fifth and last rule. Make sure that your clothes are protected by an apron and that

you're wearing nothing frilly which might catch
alight when you're leaning over a stove. And, if
you have long hair, make sure it is tied back.
I know I have gone on a bit about safety but it is
so important. After all, you want to enjoy
sweetmaking and you won't if you have even the
smallest accident.

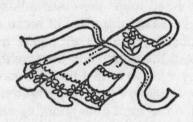

4 Sweets that don't need cooking

Having told you all about the dangers of heat, we're not at first going to use it. The recipes I start with are for some sweets that need no cooking, only mixing. Of course, one of the differences between them and cooked sweets is that they don't keep so long. But then no sweets keep very long! I remember when we were young we used to say that we'd make them last, but somehow our good intentions and our sweets seemed to fade away quickly. It's funny how often you hear people who have cooked things saying that they don't fancy eating them. It's a complaint I've never suffered from.

On the other hand, and this may surprise you, I have got tired of factory-made sweets. It was like this. I left school when I was thirteen. I took one or two odd jobs before I decided to go in for domestic work. One of these was serving in a sweet-shop. It was part-time from nine in the morning until two in the afternoon. The lady who owned the shop said when she offered me the job that I could eat as many sweets as I liked. Well, I thought I was in Aladdin's cave. Ali Baba had nothing on me. At first I sampled all the treasures I could see but then, after about a week, I just didn't want to know. The idea of eating a sweet sickened me. But of course my

-TREACLE TOFFEE-   -LUCKY BAGS-

brothers and sisters knew where I was working and came along to spend their pocket money. They were given a penny a week and even though they could get quite a bit for that, they made up to me and I'd give them more than they should have had. Then they'd bring their friends along and I'd treat them the same way. Well I knew I shouldn't have done it, but once I'd started it wasn't easy to stop. I was found out and got the sack. I learnt two things – not to cheat the person I was working for, and that things you can have for nothing aren't worth very much.

Now, here's what you've been waiting for. The doing, the recipes . . .

Orange Creams

You will need:

Icing sugar	400 grams (1 lb)
Cream of tartar	
Lemon juice	½ teaspoon
1 orange	

You make it this way:

If there are any lumps in the icing sugar, crush them with a rolling pin, or rub through a wire sieve. Put the sugar and a pinch of cream of tartar into the large basin. Grate the orange rind on to the sugar, add the lemon juice and a little of the orange juice.

Make sure that your hands are very clean, then work the ingredients together with your hands into a firm, smooth mass. This is quite hard work, so don't despair. If it won't keep together, keep adding a little more orange juice until it does.

Take care not to add too much juice or you will find that instead of a firm, smooth mass, you have a wet, sticky mess. When you get the mixture just right, turn it on to a marble slab if your mother has one; if not, put it on a pastry board. Roll it out until it's about 3 mm (⅛ inch) thick – it won't matter if it's a bit thicker. If the rolling pin sticks to the mixture, dust it lightly with a little icing sugar.

Lay out a large sheet of greaseproof paper; cut the orange creams into small rounds with a cutter and leave them to dry and harden. When they are dry on one side (after several hours), turn them over. If you are going to pack them into a box, put greaseproof paper between each layer. These sweets are very 'more-ish' but don't eat them all in one day.

Coffee Almond Creams

You will need:

Icing sugar   400 grams (1 lb)
Coffee essence
1 egg-white
Almonds

You make it this way:

Do the same with the icing sugar as in the previous recipe. Add a little coffee essence to flavour the sweets. You can either use the coffee essence that can be bought in a bottle, or make a little very strong coffee using the instant powder.

To separate the egg-white from the yolk, carefully crack the egg on the side of the cup and break it open gently so that the yolk is in one half of the shell. Let the white run out from the other half, tip the yolk into this and the rest of the white will run out. Put the yolk into another cup; your mother will be able to use it later, in her cooking. If you are unlucky and break the yolk into the white, then you will have to eat the

27

egg for your breakfast the next morning and try again with another; let's hope eggs are cheap that week.

Beat the egg-white just a little with a fork and add a small amount at a time to the bowl of sugar and coffee. You must be careful when adding both the egg-white and coffee not to put too much in. Work it all together with your hands until it is one piece but *not* wet and sticky, then turn it on to a slab or board. Sprinkle the board with icing sugar and work the piece of coffee cream until it looks smooth. Shape it into small balls, and press an almond into the top of each. (If your almonds are not bought already skinned, then put them into a basin and pour over hot water. In a few minutes you will find that the skins will easily rub off.)

Leave the sweet balls to set.

Peppermint Creams

You will need:

Icing sugar   400 grams (1 lb)
Whites of 2 medium eggs
Oil of peppermint

You make it this way:

Prepare the sugar as in the previous recipes. The
white of the two medium eggs must be whipped
to a froth with a fork. Add these bit by bit to the
icing sugar, with a few drops of oil of peppermint, until the mixture just holds together.

Using your hands, mix this to a stiff paste. If it
seems too dry, add a few drops of water.
Sprinkle the pastry board or slab with icing
sugar, put the paste on to this and roll out to
about 12 mm (½ inch) thickness. Use a small
cutter to make rounds with and leave to get
hard. This will take about a day.

If you are packing any of these cream sweets into
a box, don't have a tight-fitting lid or the sweets
won't keep for long.

5 Toffee

Making toffee is a very pleasant way of passing the time, especially if you are on holiday from school and it's raining. My children regularly had what they called 'our toffee afternoon' and, my goodness, they certainly produced some peculiar kinds of toffee. They would insist on making up their own recipes, which they considered an improvement on mine. So I would find that they had made toffee flavoured with, for example, caraway seeds – which to my mind certainly didn't make it more eatable.

One Saturday afternoon they really excelled themselves. I had to go out, so I left them in the charge of my sister. She was their favourite aunt; mainly because she was so fond of them that she let them do practically anything they liked. Maybe I should have left strict instructions about what they could or could not do. I got back home about six o'clock, and to say that I was surprised at the sight of my kitchen would be an understatement.

When I was a child, my mother – who sang around the house all day – used to sing a little ditty that went like this:

Mother was stuck to the ceiling,
The kids were stuck to the floor,
Did ever you see such a family,
So stuck up before.

I was instantly reminded of this music-hall song when I saw my children that day. They certainly were stuck-up.

Their aunt had let them make toffee-apples. One of the apples, and how it got there I never did discover, was firmly stuck in the middle of the kitchen floor. When I tried to remove it from the floor by grasping the stick, it simply pulled right out of the apple. Several more apples were stuck to the kitchen table and, judging by the sticky appearance of my children, they had stuffed themselves with plenty more.

There was a strong smell of burnt toffee hanging in the air, but my children hastily assured me the toffee-apples weren't really burnt; they were meant to be that colour. Their aunt looked absolutely exhausted with 'trying to cope with three children all wanting to do the same thing,' she said. She might have been their favourite aunt, but I'm afraid they were not her favourite nephews that afternoon.

Still they set to and cleaned up. I didn't really mind about the mess because they said, 'Mum, it's been a great afternoon.' What really knocked me back was when I discovered that they had chopped up all my carefully hoarded pistachio nuts. Those nuts really were expensive. They had stuck them all over the toffee-apples to 'make them look different'. They certainly succeeded in that.

Treacle Candy

You will need:

Golden syrup	200 grams (8 oz)
Soft brown sugar	150 grams (6 oz)
Butter	30 grams (1 oz)
Lemon juice	1 dessertspoon
Vinegar	1 teaspoon
Bicarbonate of soda	½ teaspoon

You make it this way:

Put the golden syrup, sugar, butter and lemon
juice into a pan, place over a low heat and bring
to the boil, stirring it from time to time. For the
next part I think that you should get your mother
or an older person to help you. When the
mixture has reached boiling point, test from time
to time to see if the toffee will set. To do this,
drop a little from your wooden spoon into a
saucer of cold water. If the toffee hardens quickly
in the water, it is ready. At this point remove it
from the heat.

Put the vinegar into a cup and stir the bicarbonate into it. Add this to the mixture in the pan, stir well, then pour into an oiled or greased tin. You can oil the tin with a little olive- or salad-oil. As the edges of the candy begin to cool, stir them into the mixture so that it all cools down together. As soon as the mixture is cool enough to handle, take it out of the tin and form it into a roll. Get your mother to help you: keep pulling, folding and working the candy until it turns a lighter colour and goes stiff. Finish by pulling into strips and mark these with a knife; when quite cold it can be broken into pieces at the places where you have marked it.

Everton Toffee

You will need:

Butter or margarine	125 grams (4½ oz)
Soft brown sugar	300 grams (12 oz)
Golden syrup	2 tablespoons
Water	¹⁄₁₆ litre (⅛ pint)

You make it this way:

Put all the ingredients into a pan, bring to the boil, then let it boil gently for 25 to 30 minutes, stirring from time to time. Test as for the previous recipe – ie, drop a little of the mixture into a saucer of cold water, and if the droplet snaps when you take it out of the water and breaks easily, it is ready. Do not boil over a high flame or the toffee will become too dark. When it is ready, pour into an oiled tin; as it begins to cool mark with a knife and when cold break into squares. Wrap each piece in greaseproof paper.

Chocolate Toffee

You will need:

Plain chocolate   100 grams (4 oz)
Milk   ¼ litre (½ pint)
Granulated sugar   200 grams (8 oz)
(You could use chocolate powder instead of a bar of chocolate)

You make it this way:

Grate the chocolate into a basin and mix with a little of the milk, warmed, until it is quite smooth. Put the rest of the milk into a pan with the sugar; stir over a low heat until the sugar is dissolved, then stir in the chocolate mixture. Boil gently until the toffee thickens, stirring fairly often; test for setting, as in previous recipe. Pour into an oiled tin, mark into squares and leave until it sets. If you want to make nut chocolate toffee, stir in some chopped peanuts, as you are boiling the toffee.

Coconut Toffee

You will need:

Demerara sugar	300 grams (12 oz)
Butter or margarine	90 grams (3½ oz)
Coconut (desiccated)	60 grams (just over 2 oz)

Lemon juice

You make it this way:

Put the sugar and butter into a pan, place on a low heat and stir until the sugar has dissolved; add the coconut and a few drops of lemon juice, turn the heat up and quickly bring to the boil. Test it for setting as for previous toffee recipes. When ready, pour into an oiled tin, mark into squares and leave until set.

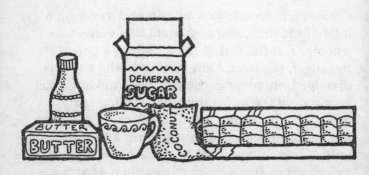

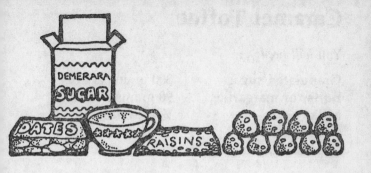

Date or Raisin Toffee

You will need:

Stoned dates	200 grams (8 oz) *or*
Seeded raisins	200 grams (8 oz)
Demerara sugar	300 grams (12 oz)
Water	1 teacup

You make it this way:

Slightly warm the fruit in the oven (if you are using dates, chop them roughly first). Put the sugar and water into a pan and stir over a low heat until the sugar has dissolved. Bring to the boil and let it boil for 10 to 15 minutes. Remove from the heat, stir until the mixture thickens, add the warmed dates or raisins and beat well until the contents become really thick. Put small heaps on to an oiled tin and leave until cold.

Caramel Toffee

You will need:

Granulated sugar	300 grams (12 oz)
Butter or margarine	90 grams (3½ oz)
Milk	¼ breakfast-cup
Golden syrup	¼ breakfast-cup
Vanilla essence	

You make it this way:

Put all the ingredients except the vanilla into a pan, place over a low heat and bring to the boil, stirring occasionally. Cook slowly for 25 to 30 minutes. Drop a little into cold water; if it forms a soft ball, remove from heat and stir in a few drops of vanilla essence. Pour all into an oiled tin, mark into toffee-sized squares with a knife and leave until cold. Break into squares where the knife marks are and wrap in greaseproof paper.

Toffee-Apples

For the toffee you will need:

Demerara sugar	400 grams (1 lb)
Water	⅛ litre (¼ pint)
Golden syrup	150 grams (6 oz)
Butter	50 grams (2 oz)
Juice of 1 small lemon	

You will also need:

As many apples as you want to make into toffee-apples and the same number of sticks. These must be strong enough to stick into and support the apple, and not less than 10 cm (4 in) long. Wooden skewers or thin sticks from a gardening shop, broken to the right lengths, would do. I used to buy small Cox's apples; but if you prefer a sourer apple, cheap cooking-apples would do. If you are not going to peel the apples, do remember to wash them well. If you do like them peeled, then after you have removed the skin, keep the apples in a bowl of cold water

until you are ready to dip them in the toffee.
Otherwise, the apples will turn brown.

You make the toffee this way:

Put the sugar and water into a pan and place
over a low heat. When the sugar has dissolved,
add the Golden syrup and butter, bring to the
boil, stirring all the time. Test for setting as in
previous recipes. When ready remove from heat,
add the lemon juice and as quickly as possible
dip each apple into the toffee until well coated.
Place on greased dish to set.

6 Fudge

I am sure that you will enjoy making, and eating, fudge. It is one of my favourite sweets. It is also the kind of rather 'gooey' sweet that sticks in your teeth. If we were given a piece to eat just before we went to bed, my mother always made sure that we brushed our teeth afterwards. It wasn't any use pretending that we had, because sometimes she would carry out an 'inspection parade', as Mother called it. We never knew what night she would do this so we didn't dare to skip the teeth-brushing.

Mum sometimes let us make sweets on a Saturday morning. Mind you, we all had to do our share of the household chores before we could enjoy ourselves. I always reckoned that because I was a girl, and the eldest girl too, I had to do more work than any of the others. All that my brothers had to do was to run errands. I say run but, judging by the time it took them to go to the corner shop and back, they must have crawled.

One of my Saturday morning jobs was cleaning the brass stair-rods. I very much disliked doing this as not only did my hands get filthy, but I couldn't bear the smell of brass polish. Neither was I keen on washing up the breakfast things. In fact the only job that I really enjoyed doing was cleaning the windows. The reason why I liked this job was because our windows weren't cleaned with a wash-leather. I had a bucket of cold water and a large syringe, which I filled with the cold water and then squirted all over the windows. It was great fun. Especially so when I did the top windows and all the water ran down the house. Though it wasn't much fun one morning when I forgot to shut the bedroom window, and a great stream of water went over my mother's bed. You can be certain that I didn't mention sweetmaking on that morning.

We used to take our home-made sweets to the pictures. Saturday afternoons were for children only, though mothers could go if their children were very young. Very few mothers braved the pictures on a Saturday afternoon. The noise was too much for them. As they were silent films in those days, with just a few words shown on the screen to tell you how the story was getting along, it didn't matter how the children talked and bawled out to each other from one side of the cinema to the other. We sat downstairs. It cost less than 1p to sit there and about 1½p to sit in the gallery. The lucky children who sat up there used to bombard us down below with sweet wrappers, apple cores and orange peel.

I remember one Saturday afternoon three of us set out for the pictures, each carrying a bag of nut fudge. My mother insisted on sharing out the sweets equally before we left home, just in case we quarrelled over who was to carry the bag.

During the main picture, when the heroine was tied to the railway line and the train was coming ever nearer and nearer, I dropped my bag of fudge on the floor in the excitement. I didn't miss it until it was time for the interval. By that time the bag had been trodden on by a dozen or more boots. The contents looked like a flat brown pancake. Nevertheless, as the bag had not broken, I still ate the fudge. I must admit that it seemed to taste a bit more gritty than usual.

Chocolate Fudge

You will need:

Granulated sugar	400 grams (1 lb)
Butter	25 grams (1 oz)
Condensed milk (unsweetened)	¼ litre (½ pint)
Plain chocolate	125 grams (5 oz)
Water	2 tablespoons
Vanilla essence	1 teaspoon

You make it this way:

Put all the ingredients except the vanilla essence into a pan. You will need a fairly large one. Stand the pan on a low heat until the sugar has melted. Then turn up the heat and boil fairly rapidly for 25 to 30 minutes. Don't forget to stir occasionally in case the sugar is sticking to the bottom of the pan. Then, take the pan off the heat, stir in the vanilla essence and beat the mixture with a wooden spoon until it thickens and looks creamy. Turn it out as quickly as possible on to a greased tin. When it is almost

cold, cut the fudge into pieces with a sharp knife
– be careful when you use this. When the fudge
is quite cold, turn it out of the tin on to a piece
of greaseproof paper. After a short time, pack it
away into a tin – if you haven't eaten it all before
then.

Raspberry Dreams

You will need:

Raspberries	200 grams (½ lb)
Gelatine	¾ oz
Loaf sugar	400 grams (1 lb)
Icing sugar	

You make it this way:

Put the raspberries into a pan and cover with
cold water. Cook until soft and the juice can be
squeezed from them. Put them into a piece of
clean cloth and squeeze over a bowl until all the
juice has been extracted. Add enough water to
the juice to make the liquid up to ¼ litre (½
pint). Put back into the pan, add the sugar, bring
to the boil and boil quickly for about two
minutes. Remove from heat, add the gelatine,
stir until dissolved. Dip a shallow tin into cold
water, then pour in the raspberry mixture. When
quite cold turn on to a board previously
sprinkled with icing sugar and cut into squares,
coating each piece with the icing sugar. Leave for
a day or two to dry, then pack into a box.

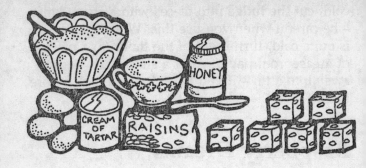

Honey Fudge

You will need:

Granulated sugar	3 teacups
Honey	1½ teacups
Water	1 tablespoon
Cream of tartar	
3 egg-whites	
Seedless raisins	50 grams (2 oz)

You make it this way:

Put the sugar, honey and water into a pan, place over a low heat until the sugar has dissolved. Add a pinch of cream of tartar and boil gently until it forms a soft ball if you put a little into cold water. Leave on a very low heat.

Separate the three egg-whites from the yolks. For an easy way to do this, see the recipe for coffee almond creams on page 27. Put the egg-whites in a medium-sized bowl and whip to a stiff froth with a rotary whisk. They must be so stiff that if you turn the basin upside-down the egg-whites will not drop out. Pour the fudge mixture on to the egg-whites, stir in the raisins, and beat until it becomes thick and creamy. Pour into a greased tin and when almost cold cut into squares. Pack into greaseproof paper when quite cold.

Nut Fudge

You will need:

Milk	⅛ litre (¼ pint)
Granulated sugar	350 grams (14 oz)
Butter	25 grams (1 oz)
Chopped walnuts	50 grams (2 oz)
Vanilla essence	

You make it this way:

Put the sugar and milk into a pan, place over a low heat and bring to the boil. Leave on a low heat, test at intervals to see if ready. To test: drop a small piece into a basin of cold water;

when it forms into a soft ball the mixture is
ready. Remove from the heat, add the butter,
half of the nuts and about ½ teaspoon of vanilla
essence and beat with a wooden spoon until the
mixture thickens. Pour into a tin lined with
greased greaseproof paper and before completely
cold mark into squares and decorate with the rest
of the walnuts.

7 Marzipan

Some of the prettiest sweets can be made with marzipan. It's not too difficult to use different liquid colourings (these can be bought cheaply at any good grocer's), or to shape the marzipan into fruits. For instance, if you want to make apple or pear shapes, put a clove in one end to look like a stalk. Of course you don't eat the clove. You can colour the marzipan by putting a few drops of colouring in and mixing it with your hands on a board before you shape the fruit. Or, you can make the fruits first and then, using a small clean paint-brush, you can paint them with the colouring first diluted with a little water. If you were making marzipan oranges, in miniature of course, after you have made the shapes, roll them on a nutmeg-grater or fine sieve. This will make a rough surface, like orange peel. If you want to make leaves, then work a little green colouring into the marzipan; make sure that the colour is evenly mixed in. Roll out on a board sprinkled with sugar and cut into leaf shapes.

If you pack alternate colours into a box it makes a very nice birthday present. The stationery departments of most large stores stock fancy sweet-cases and coloured paper. If you have a fancy box, put a layer of paper shavings at the bottom, then a piece of greaseproof paper the

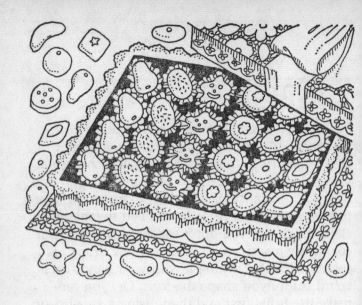

same size as the box. You can put strips of greaseproof paper between the rows of sweets; you must certainly put a piece between each layer. When you have filled your box, put on a piece of greaseproof paper to cover right over, than another layer of paper shavings. Use enough to prevent the sweets from rattling when you put on the lid. Lastly, if you have any spare ribbon, tie this round the box and finish with a bow.

There are two ways of making marzipan: cooked and uncooked. If you want to keep the marzipan a long time it is probably better to use the cooked method, but uncooked marzipan is very easy and quite suitable if it is to be eaten soon.

Uncooked Marzipan

You will need:

Icing sugar	75 grams (3 oz)
Ground almonds	150 grams (6 oz)
Caster sugar	75 grams (3 oz)
2 egg-whites	
Almond essence	

You make it this way:

Sift the icing sugar and put it into a bowl with the caster sugar and ground almonds. Lightly beat the whites of two medium-sized eggs and add a few drops of almond essence. Pour half of this into the bowl and, using your hands, work the mixture together. Add the rest of the egg-white a little at a time until it all clings together and is made into a firm paste. (If you want to know an easy way to separate the white from the yolk, turn to the recipe for coffee almond creams on page 27).

Cooked Marzipan

As this will keep for several months it is worth making a fair amount in one go.

You will need:

Granulated sugar	400 grams (1 lb)
Water	⅛ litre (¼ pint)
Cream of tartar	⅛ teaspoon
Ground almonds	300 grams (12 oz)
Almond essence	
2 egg-whites	

You make it this way:

Put the sugar and water into a pan and leave it to soak for an hour. Then put over a low heat until the sugar has dissolved. Bring to the boil, add the cream of tartar and let the mixture boil for 5 minutes. Remove from the heat, stir in the ground almonds and a few drops of the essence. Let it cool for a few minutes, then add the lightly beaten whites and mix well. Sprinkle a board with caster sugar, turn the marzipan on to it and, using your hands, knead the mixture well. When it is cold, wrap in greaseproof paper and pack in an air-tight tin.

Now that you know how to make marzipan, here are three marzipan sweet recipes:

Marzipan Dates

All that you will need for this is marzipan and dates. But you must have the right kind of dates. Definitely not those stoneless dates that are sold in a flat pack so tightly clamped together that it looks as though a baby elephant had stood on them. When I was a child my mother told me that the natives of North Africa stamped dates into a hard mass with their bare feet. I think that perhaps she told me this to discourage me from eating too many; though I must admit that Mother always added, 'Of course they wash their feet before they start on the job.'

Anyway, what you need for this recipe is a *box* of dates. All you have to do is: remove the stones (a

somewhat sticky job), taking care not to cut the dates completely in half. Then roll a piece of marzipan into the same shape as the stones, but slightly larger, stuff the dates with this and close them up again.

Marzipan Delights

You will need:

Marzipan	300 grams (12 oz)
Pink colouring	
Vanilla essence	
Icing sugar	
1 egg-white	
Plain chocolate	150 grams (6 oz)

You make it this way:

Take the marzipan and divide it into two equal pieces. Colour one piece with the pink colouring and flavour the other half with a few drops of vanilla essence. Put each piece on a board that has been sprinkled with icing sugar and roll out to about ¾ inch thickness. Brush one piece with the lightly beaten egg-white and put the other piece on top. Press down firmly and leave for an hour or two. Break the chocolate into small pieces, put into a basin. Stand the basin in a pan of hot water. Leave this on a low heat until the chocolate has melted. Place the marzipan on a large plate or dish and pour the chocolate over it. Leave until it is cold and hard, then cut into small squares.

Marzipan Surprise

You will need:

Madeira cake 2 thick slices, dry enough to make into crumbs

Vanilla essence
Apricot jam
Marzipan
1 egg-white
Finely chopped walnuts

You make it this way:

Put the cake-crumbs into a basin with a few drops of vanilla essence and add jam to make the mixture stiff enough to roll into small balls. Leave these to harden overnight. Sprinkle a board with icing or caster sugar and roll out the marzipan thinly. Cut into pieces large enough to wrap round the cake-crumb balls; shape these neatly. Lightly beat the egg-white. Brush each of the marzipan balls with this and roll them in the chopped walnuts.

8 Chocolates

When my children made sweets for which they had to melt chocolate, I was always somewhat mystified to find that there never seemed to be enough chocolate. Eventually I discovered why. When they had to break the chocolate into small pieces before melting it, for every piece that went into the basin, another piece was popped into their mouths. You can be sure that after I found this out, I used to stand and watch them.

Another trouble was our ginger cat. He loved chocolate. No matter where he was, in the garden or upstairs, he always seemed to know when there was chocolate around. He would bound into the kitchen and gaze so pathetically at my children that, if they thought I wasn't looking, they would quickly give him a piece.

We had no name for our cat. He was just a stray kitten that wandered, all wet and bedraggled, into our home one day. Nobody seemed to own him. My children simply could not agree on a name for him. The youngest child wanted to call the cat Tiddles. This name made the other two hoot with laughter. My eldest son wanted to call him Horatio, because he was reading a book in which the hero was named Horatio. But our cat never looked in the least heroic. At the finish he was just a no-name cat. When we called him in

at night, we opened the door and called, 'Cat, cat, come on in, ginger-cat,' and he always came in so he must have known that was his name.

I like cats because they always seem so independent. One doesn't have to take them out for walks, neither do they gaze sorrowfully at you if you go out without them, as dogs do.

I don't know whether ginger cats are more ferocious than other coloured cats, but our cat was a great fighter. He would never let another cat into the garden, much to the annoyance of the people who shared our house. Their poor cat could never use the garden because ginger-cat always chased him away.

One day our cat got into a fight with a lean and hungry old tomcat. He was striped like a tiger.

And he fought like one too. Poor ginger-cat got half his ear bitten off. We took him to the vet who, after an examination, said that our cat would always be a bit deaf. The children spent half their pocket money – twopence each – on chocolate for ginger-cat, to console him.

The first box of chocolates that my children made was for my birthday. It was to be a surprise gift of home-made chocolate – much better than you can buy in the shops. It was a surprise all right, because they had made a mistake somehow in the making of it.

My youngest child always called soft-centre chocolates 'creamy-middles'. 'We have made you a box of chocolates with creamy-middles for your birthday, Mum,' he said. The middles were not creamy, they were liquid. Also, as they had not enough money to buy the proper wrappings, they bought a roll of orange-coloured crêpe paper and cut that up. Of course the chocolates stuck to the paper like glue. Still, I thought it was very kind of them to make the chocolates specially for me. They helped me to eat them. Those who ate most chocolates ate most paper.

By the way, if you are packing chocolates, do use brown waxed paper. Even if your efforts turn out to be perfect, and I am sure that they will after a while, chocolates do mark the paper. On white waxed paper you will find that the chocolates leave a nasty mark.

Chocolate Peppermints

You will need:

White fat	25 grams (1 oz)
Powdered glucose	50 grams (2 oz)
Boiling water	2 tablespoons
1 egg-white	
Icing sugar	450 grams (18 oz)
Peppermint essence	
Green colouring	
Plain chocolate	100 grams (4 oz)

You make it this way:

Put the white fat (Cookeen will do for this) into a basin, add the glucose and boiling water. Beat well together. Separate the yolk from the white of a standard-size egg, put the white into a cup, lightly beat it and add to the glucose mixture. Make sure that you are using a large basin because now you have to beat in the icing sugar gradually until the mixture forms a paste. You may find that you do not need all of the sugar – it should be about as firm as pastry before it is rolled out. Sprinkle a pastry board with icing sugar, turn out the mixture on to it and add a few drops of peppermint, mixing it in with your hands – which I hope you have washed before you start.

Be very careful about how much peppermint you use – too little is better than too much; add a few drops of green colouring by the same method. Now roll the mixture out until it is about ½ inch in thickness. Using a very small cutter, even smaller than an egg cup if you have one (if not, use an egg cup), make as many rounds as possible until you have used all the mixture. Lay them on waxed or greaseproof paper and leave until the next day. Then start again by breaking the chocolate into small pieces; put it into a basin, place the basin in a pan of hot water and leave on a low heat until the chocolate has melted. Dip the tops of the peppermints into this so that the chocolate comes about halfway up. Leave them to set for a few hours.

Chocolate Caramels

You will need:

Sweet almonds	150 grams (6 oz)
Caster sugar	200 grams (8 oz)
Water	⅛ litre (¼ pint)
Plain chocolate	150 grams (6 oz)

You make it this way:

Buy the almonds already skinned, put on to a shallow tin and brown in the oven (Gas mark 6,

Electricity 400°F or 200°C). Let them get a golden brown, remove from the oven and chop as small as you can manage.

Put the sugar into a pan, add the water, put over a low heat until the sugar has melted, then put over a higher heat and boil the sugar until it turns brown. Remove from the heat, stir in the chopped nuts and turn on to a dampened dish to cool. Before it becomes too hard, form it into balls. Break the chocolate into small pieces, put it into a basin and place the basin in a pan of hot water over a low heat. When the chocolate has melted, remove from the heat and beat until it thickens. Dip the nut balls into this and put on to a sieve, or wire tray, to dry. If you like, you could save a little of the chopped nuts to sprinkle over the balls before the chocolate has quite dried.

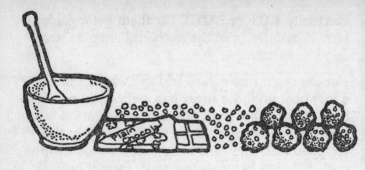

Chocolate Kisses

You will need:

Plain chocolate	100 grams (4 oz)
Chopped almonds and walnuts	50 grams (2 oz) of each

You make it this way:

Break the chocolate into small pieces, put it into a basin, place the basin in a pan of hot water over a low heat. When the chocolate is very soft, remove the basin from the pan and beat the chocolate until it is thick. Then stir in enough of the chopped nuts to make a very stiff mass – you may find that you do not need all of the nuts. You can add a few drops of vanilla essence if you like. Drop small heaps of this mixture on to a board and leave until they are hard.

Chocolate Macaroons

You will need:

Sweet almonds
Plain chocolate   150 grams (6 oz)
Packet of ratafias

You make it this way:

You may not be able to find the ratafias in a supermarket, but some grocers or high-class bakers will stock them.

Buy the almonds already skinned and lightly brown them in the oven. Split them. Put the chocolate into a basin, place this in a pan of hot water over a low heat. When the chocolate has melted, remove the basin from the pan, beat the chocolate until it thickens. Dip the ratafias into this one at a time and lay them on a large dish to harden. Just before the chocolate has quite set, put a split almond on the top.

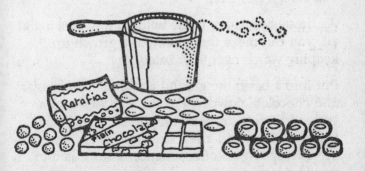

Chocolate Truffles

You will need:

Ground almonds	75 grams (3 oz)
Icing sugar	100 grams (4 oz)
Chocolate powder	1 tablespoon
1 egg-yolk	
Evaporated milk	
Coffee or vanilla essence	

You make it this way:

As these sweets are made without any cooking at all, you can make them without a grown-up keeping watch over your safety.

Put into a basin the ground almonds, icing sugar and chocolate powder. Put the egg-yolk into a cup, add a few drops of evaporated milk, beat together, then add a few drops of vanilla essence or ½ teaspoon of coffee essence. Pour this into your basin of mixture and, using your hands, mix into a soft dough. Leave this to get very cold – you could put it into the fridge for half an hour. Sprinkle a large sheet of greaseproof paper with a little more chocolate powder, or chocolate vermicelli is better to use if you have any; shape the mixture into small balls and roll them in the powder or vermicelli. If you have any paper cases, put the truffles into them.

9 Some more well-known sweets

Fresh Fruit Jellies

You will need:

Fruit juice	¼ litre (½ pint)
Gelatine	50 grams (2 oz)
Granulated sugar	200 grams (8 oz)

You make it this way:

Either buy a tin of fruit juice or, if fresh fruit such as raspberries, loganberries or blackberries are in the shops, make the juice yourself. All you do is to wash the fruit and put it into a pan. Use no water – the wetness of the fruit is enough. Put the pan over a low heat, bring to the boil, and stew gently until the fruit is soft. Then rub through a sieve or strainer.

Measure the juice, making sure that you have enough. Melt the gelatine in about half of the liquid over a low heat. Do not let it boil. In another pan put the sugar and the rest of the juice. Let the sugar dissolve over a low heat, then bring to the boil and continue to boil the syrup for about five minutes. Pour the gelatine

into this, give a good stir and boil for another two or three minutes. Rinse a shallow tin in cold water, pour in the mixture and leave until the next day, when you will be able to cut it into small squares.

Turkish Delight

You will need:

Leaf gelatine	25 grams (1 oz)
Caster sugar	400 grams (1 lb)
Water	¼ litre (½ pint)
Vanilla and raspberry flavouring	
Red colouring	
A little icing sugar and cornflour	

You make it this way:

Melt the gelatine in a little of the water over a low heat; *do not* let it boil. Put the sugar and the rest of the water into a pan over a low heat. When the sugar has dissolved add the melted gelatine. Boil this together for about 15 to 20 minutes, stirring all the time. Take it off the heat and let it stand for about 20 minutes; then divide it into warm pans. Put each on a very low heat for only a few minutes, stir well. Put a few drops of vanilla into one pan and a few drops of raspberry essence into the other; add also a few drops of colouring to this pan – enough to make it a pink shade. Moisten two shallow tins with cold water, and pour the contents of the pans into the tins; keep them separate. Leave at least 36 hours. On a large sheet of greaseproof paper mix equal amounts of icing sugar and cornflour. Cut the Turkish Delight into squares and roll these in the sugar and cornflour. Pack into a tin and sprinkle more icing sugar over.

Marshmallows

You will need:

Gelatine	25 grams (1 oz)
Granulated sugar	400 grams (1 lb)
Water	¼ litre (½ pint)
Glucose	3 teaspoons
2 egg-whites	
A little icing sugar and	
** cornflour**	

You make it this way:

Melt the gelatine in a little of the water but *do not* let it boil. Put the sugar into a pan with the rest of the water, add the glucose, bring to the boil and keep it boiling for about three minutes. Then pour this into the pan containing the melted gelatine. Beat the egg-whites into a very stiff froth, add the gelatine mixture and beat the mixture well together. It should become thick and creamy. Sprinkle an oiled tin with a little icing sugar and cornflour and put the marshmallow into this; leave for several hours. Turn out on to a board sprinkled with sugar and cornflour, cut into squares and coat with the sugar mixture. Pack in greaseproof paper.

Almond Pralines

You will need:

Almonds	200 grams (8 oz)
Granulated sugar	400 grams (1 lb)
Water	⅛ litre (¼ pint)
Almond essence	

You make it this way:

If the almonds are not already skinned, pour hot water over them, leave for a few minutes, and then the skins will be easy to remove. Brown them to a golden colour in the oven. Be careful not to overbrown. Put the sugar and the water into a pan and place over a low heat. When it starts to boil, add the almonds, then let it boil until the syrup becomes a pale brown colour. Keep stirring all the time. Remove from the heat,

add a few drops of almond essence and shake the pan gently to mix the essence well. If you have a marble slab, place the almond mixture in small heaps on this, using a tablespoon. If you don't possess one, then lightly oil a tin and use in the same way.

Almond Brazils

You will need:

Ground almonds	100 grams (4 oz)
Icing sugar	100 grams (4 oz)
Almond essence	
Butter	25 grams (1 oz)
Granulated sugar	100 grams (4 oz)
Water	1 tablespoon
Brazil nuts	

(bought ready shelled, or you can shell your own)

You make it this way:

Put the ground almonds and the icing sugar into a basin, add a few drops of almond essence. Rub in the butter and form the mixture into a paste. If it seems too dry add a few drops of milk. Put the granulated sugar into a pan with the water and place over a low heat until it boils. Cover each Brazil nut with some of the almond paste; make it into a neat shape. Then, using a steel skewer, pick them up one at a time and dip them into the boiling syrup. As you do each one lay it on a sieve, or a wire tray, to dry.

Honey Popcorn

You will need:

Butter	50 grams (2 oz)
Popcorn kernels	3 tablespoons
Clear honey	3 tablespoons

You make it this way:

It's fun to make this sweet, as you can hear the corn popping away in the pan. Put three-quarters of the butter into a large pan and place over a low heat until the butter has melted. Then sprinkle the corn into the pan – it should be large enough for the corn just to cover the base – put on the lid, which should fit tightly, and place the pan over a moderate heat. Every now and again give the pan a shake and soon you will hear the corn popping. Keep on giving a shake but do not take off the lid until you can no longer hear the corn popping; then remove the pan from the heat. Put the rest of the butter into a large frying pan (if you can add a little more, it will improve the popcorn), add the honey, heat until the butter has melted, tip in the popcorn and stir in gently but well. Turn out on to a lightly greased plate and leave to cool.

Peppermint Drops

You will need:

Granulated sugar	400 grams (1 lb)
Water	⅛ litre (¼ pint)
Cream of tartar	
Peppermint essence	

You make it this way:

Put the sugar and water into a pan, place over a low heat until the sugar has dissolved, then add a pinch of cream of tartar and let it boil quickly for about 10 to 12 minutes. Remove from the heat, add a few drops of peppermint essence and stir well. Leave the mixture to cool a little, then, using a wooden spoon, beat it until it becomes creamy. Using a dessertspoon, drop the mixture in small heaps on to an oiled tin or marble slab. Leave them until they harden.

Coconut Ice

You will need:

Granulated sugar	400 grams (1 lb)
Water	1 teacup
Desiccated coconut	100 grams (4 oz)
Peppermint or vanilla flavouring	
Condensed milk	2 tablespoons
Pink colouring	

You make it this way:

Put the sugar and water into a pan and place over a low heat until the sugar has melted. Then let it boil for about 10 minutes. Remove from the heat, add the coconut and a few drops of peppermint or vanilla flavouring. Put back on to the heat and let it boil for about 10 minutes, but this time you must keep on stirring the mixture. When it has thickened, remove from the heat and stir in the condensed milk. Mix this well, then pour half of it into a tin that you have already greased with butter. Add a few drops of pink colouring to the other half of the mixture, stir this well and pour it over the white half in the tin.

Leave until it is cold and firm, then cut it into small oblong pieces. You can wrap the coconut ice in greaseproof paper; but it will not keep for a long time.

Coconut Balls

You will need:

Granulated sugar	300 grams (12 oz)
Water	⅛ litre (¼ pint)
Desiccated coconut	125 grams (5 oz)
Any flavouring that you like	
Colouring	

You make it this way:

Melt the sugar and water over a low heat and then let it boil for about 10 minutes. Remove from the heat and add the coconut; then boil it for another 10 minutes, stirring it all the time. Meanwhile, have ready a large basin of hot water and stand a smaller basin in it. When the coconut mixture has thickened, remove it from the heat, put some in the smaller basin, flavour it (only a few drops) and then add a few drops of whatever colour you like. Form into balls about the size of a walnut, roll them in desiccated coconut and stand on a sieve or tray to dry. Use the rest of the mixture in the same way. If you use different colourings and flavourings the sweets look very nice when placed in a box together.

Coconut Pyramids

You will need:

3 egg-whites
Caster sugar	175 grams (7 oz)
Desiccated coconut	200 grams (8 oz)

You make it this way:

I have told you in an earlier recipe how to separate the yolks from the whites of the eggs.* But as you are using three eggs for this recipe, it is a good idea, after you have separated the first egg, to do the other two one at a time into a cup. Otherwise, if you put the first egg-white into the basin and break the others over it, calamity might be the result. For should any of the yolks get into the white you will not be able to whip them to a very stiff froth.

When you have all three whites safely in the basin (you will need to use a fairly large one), they must be whipped to such a stiff froth that when you turn the basin upside-down the froth doesn't drop out. I don't advise you to try this unless your mother has inspected it, if it's the first time you have tried. I do all my whipping with just an ordinary hand whisk. Your mother may have an electric mixer, but she may not think that you are experienced enough to use it.

Continue with the recipe by stirring in the coconut and sugar. Put a piece of greased paper on to a fairly large, flat tin and put the coconut mixture on this in small lumps – about the size of a walnut.

Bake in a moderate oven for 20 to 30 minutes; the pyramids should be a pale brown when done.

Gas mark 4 to 5, Electricity 350°–375°F or 180°–190°C.

* See Coffee Almond Creams, page 27.

10 Fondants

Fondant is perhaps more difficult to make than some of the other recipes in this book. So it might be a good idea to start on the simpler sweets until you feel really confident. Fondant can be cooked or uncooked and both types should be wrapped in greaseproof paper or foil until required. You might find, if fondant has been kept for some time, that it has become too hard. If so it's quite simple to put right. All you do is to put the fondant into a basin, then stand the basin in a pan of hot water until the fondant is warm. You will then be able to mould it into any shapes that you like.

As well as being a nice sweet to eat on its own, fondant is so handy for use in other sweets. It can be used to stuff dates, first removing the stones, or it can be used for the centre of chocolates, coloured and flavoured in any way that you fancy. Put between layers of marzipan, it makes a delicious sweet bar. I have even used it on the top of cakes instead of icing.

The uncooked type of fondant is very simple to make. After kneading it well, wrap in greaseproof paper and set it aside for two days before using. The only drawback to uncooked fondant is that, after a few days it becomes very hard and breaks up when you try to use it.

Cooked fondant keeps fresh for a much longer time. So it really is worth the extra trouble because you can make a large amount and then store it for use in the future. Don't let the term 'kneading' put you off; all it means is mixing with your hands; then when you have the mixture in a lump, keep on moulding it together, using your knuckles as much as possible.

Years and years ago, when I was only nine years old, we had a baker on the corner of our street who baked all his bread in his own bakehouse in the basement under the shop. The most delicious smells used to float through the grating in the pavement. If he was in a good mood he would let me go into the basement and watch the men kneading the dough. I expect that nowadays all kneading is done by machinery. But our baker's men kneaded with their hands. They would knuckle, slap and punch around enormous masses of dough as though it was as light as a feather. I must admit the bread was like that after it was cooked. Lovely bread, one could eat it just as it was, it didn't matter about margarine or butter. The heat in that bakehouse was almost beyond description. The men were sweating, as red as turkey-cocks and forever wiping their shining faces with a damp cloth.

Whenever we made sweets that involved using
our hands, my mother always carried out an
inspection of them. Our idea of clean hands was
just a hurried rinse with cold water and a quick
wipe on the towel. That didn't do for my
mother. She carried out an inspection before we
started on the sweetmaking; if our nails were
dirty we were promptly told to scrub them with
the nail brush. My brothers and I used to
grumble about all this cleanliness – but we never
let Mum hear us. We used to say, 'We might just
as well be in school,' where the teachers had a
hand inspection every morning. Our teacher
would line us up in rows – all fifty of us – with
our hands stretched out in front. Then she would
walk up and down the rows like a sergeant-
major. She always carried a ruler, a hard wooden
one, and if she found a girl with grubby hands,

that girl got a hard whack with this ruler. I can tell you, it wasn't at all pleasant, and in some cases very unfair. For most of us lived in places without a bathroom and just one cold-water tap in the kitchen. It was far from easy to get one's turn at the sink.

Mind you, although we thought that our Mum was too fussy over this hand-washing, I found that when I became a Mum, I was just the same. And my children grumbled in the same way. The only difference was that they didn't mind if I heard them.

Another thing that my Mum insisted on was that we all wore an apron of some kind. As my Dad's trade was painting and decorating, we used to borrow his painters' aprons. They had very large

bibs. I can see now why Mum made us wear them. For children's clothes in those days were not made of the 'easy-to-wash' material that we can buy today. When I went to school I wore thick serge frocks – terribly itchy the stuff was too. On top of that I wore white starched pinafores with shoulder frills. However hard I tried, I could never keep these white pinafores clean for more than two days. So, as there were no washing-machines then, it used to take our Mum all day to do the washing in a large wooden tub. I always disliked washing-day, because often Mum kept me home from school to help her. I much preferred to be at school; I really liked all the lessons except the needlework.

Plain Uncooked Fondant

You will need:

Icing sugar
Glucose   1 teaspoon
Boiling water   1 tablespoon

You make it this way:

If you have a wire sieve, put the sugar through
it. If you have no sieve, make sure that there are
no lumps in the sugar. Mix the glucose with the
water, put into a basin and add the icing sugar a
little at a time, stirring it well. Keep on adding
sugar, stirring and beating, until all the water is
used up; the mixture should be dry enough to
handle. Sprinkle a board with icing sugar, put
the fondant on to it, and knead it until it is quite
smooth. Leave it for two to three hours, covered
with greaseproof paper.

Plain Cooked Fondant

You will need:

Granulated sugar	400 grams (1 lb)
Water	$\frac{1}{10}$ litre (7½ fluid oz)
Glucose	2 teaspoons

You make it this way:

Put the sugar and water into a pan, place over a
low heat and stir until the sugar has melted.
Then add the glucose and quickly bring the
mixture to the boil. Let it keep boiling until,
when you drop a little piece into cold water, it
forms a soft ball when you rub it between your
fingers. When it is ready, let it cool slightly. Now
you really need a marble slab for the next step,
but if you haven't got one, a heavy board will
do. Slightly moisten the marble slab or board
with water, pour the mixture on to it and, using
a broad-bladed knife, fold the outsides of the
mixture into the centre. Do this several times.
When the mixture is cool enough to handle,
sprinkle icing sugar on your hands and keep on
kneading the mixture until it is very smooth,

white and creamy. You can add any flavourings or colourings that you like; it's best to do this while the mixture is still warm. Let the mixture stand for two to three hours, covered with a clean, damp cloth. You can then roll it into any small shapes that you fancy.

Now that you can make cooked and uncooked fondant, here are four sweet recipes which use fondant:

Coconut Cream Fondant

You will need:

Icing sugar	400 grams (1 lb)
Cream of tartar	
Cream	2 tablespoons
1 egg-white	
Desiccated coconut	150 grams (6 oz)

You make it this way:

Put the icing sugar through a wire sieve; or crush
all lumps with a rolling pin. Put it into a large
basin, add a pinch of cream of tartar and the
cream. Lightly beat the egg-white and add just
enough to the mixture to form it into a thick
paste. Let it stand for about three hours. Mix in
the coconut, turn on to a board sprinkled with
icing sugar, knead it well, then roll out and cut
the fondant into cubes. In a few hours it will
harden.

Chocolate Walnut Fondant

You will need:

Uncooked fondant	300 grams (12 oz)
Plain chocolate	75 grams (3 oz)
Cream	$\frac{1}{16}$ litre ($\frac{1}{8}$ pint)
Chopped walnuts	

You make it this way:

Prepare the fondant as in the recipe for plain uncooked fondant*; it should be left for at least two hours before being used.

Break the chocolate into small pieces, put into a basin and place the basin in a pan of hot water to melt the chocolate. When it has melted, let it cool a little, then stir in the cream. Sprinkle a board with icing sugar, roll out the fondant on this and pour a little of the chocolate over it. Knead the mixture, roll out again and add more chocolate. Continue to roll and knead until all the chocolate

* See page 83.

has been used in the fondant. Make into rough lumps, more or less all the same size, place these on the board and sprinkle with the chopped walnuts.

Coffee Walnut Fondant

You will need:

Fondant	300 grams (12 oz)
Shelled walnuts	75 grams (3 oz)
Coffee essence	
1 egg-white	

You make it this way:

Prepare the fondant as in the recipe for plain cooked fondant*. Chop the walnuts. Sprinkle a board with icing sugar, roll out the fondant on this, pour about a ½ teaspoonful of coffee essence in the middle. Fold the sides of the fondant towards the centre and knead it until the coffee is mixed in well. If the fondant has not turned a coffee colour, add enough essence to make it do this, kneading all the time. Then form into small balls, brush over with the egg-white and roll them in the chopped walnuts. Make sure that they are well coated with the nuts.

*See page 84.

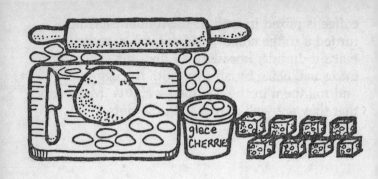

Cherry and Almond Fondant

You will need:

Fondant	about 200 grams (8 oz)
Glacé cherries	75 grams (3 oz)
Almonds	50 grams (2 oz)

You make it this way:

Make the fondant as in the recipe for plain cooked fondant*. Put the cherries on to a board sprinkled with icing sugar, and chop them into small pieces. If the almonds are not already skinned, remove the skins and chop them rather finely. Sprinkle the board with more icing sugar, roll the fondant out to a large, fairly thin piece. Sprinkle the chopped almonds and cherries over this, fold the sides of the fondant over the fruit and nuts and knead it well. When you have thoroughly mixed it, roll it out again to about 2.5 cm (1 in) in thickness. Cut into cubes, roll these in icing sugar. They will take about three hours to harden.

*See page 84.

Index

edited by Biddy Baxter
The Blue Peter Book of Gorgeous Grub 95p

When the *Blue Peter* BBC television programme launched its Gorgeous Grub competition, children sent in 33,250 of their own favourite recipes. Here are the forty prizewinners, a collection of mouth-watering gorgeous grub! A part of the publisher's profits from the sale of this book were donated to the International Year of the Child.

Marguerite Patten
The Piccolo Cook Book 60p

If you enjoy cooking you should have this book from this well-known cookery writer. You will find you are able to delight and surprise your friends and family with delicious dishes and even whole meals. *The Piccolo Cook Book* is jam-packed with step-by-step instructions, advice on utensils needed and practical recipes which are simple to follow and fun to prepare.

Vladimir Koziakin
Superworld Mazes 95p

The Cybourg missions have attacked the human colonies – you
have 4 minutes 45 seconds to get them out of danger! Which
route? Can you do it? Will you be able to save the humans or will
they fall into the evil clutches of rogue Cybourgs, or plunge deep
into the whirling vortex of space? It's a risk – solve the maze
puzzles and you will live to fight again.

compiled by Nigel Blundel
Sick as a Parrot 95p

The worst of the best sick jokes you will find – our author has
made himself very sick collecting them. You will feel ill, scream,
bang your head and lose your friends if you repeat these jokes.
Take care – you have been warned! This book is not for the
squeamish!

You can buy these and other Piccolo books from booksellers and
newsagents; or direct from the following address:
Pan Books, Sales Office, Cavaye Place, London SW10 9PG
Send purchase price plus 35p for the first book and 15p for
each additional book, to allow for postage and packing.
Prices quoted are applicable in the UK

While every effort is made to keep prices low, it is sometimes
necessary to increase prices at short notice. Pan Books reserve
the right to show on covers and charge new retail prices which
may differ from those advertised in the text or elsewhere